*Little Inventions*

# FRENCH FRIES

RAPHAËL FEJTÖ

FIREFLY BOOKS

Legend has it that in 1828, Jean Frédéric
Krieger, a young German born into a family
of fairground musicians, left for Paris to learn

how to cook and started working in a restaurant in Montmartre. There, the head chef let him in on his specialty dish.

They were potatoes cut into rounds and then thrown into grease and fried until they became golden and crispy.

Jean Frédéric thought they were so good, he decided to sell them on the street. They were a hit!

Since he had made a lot of money, he decided to go back to the country to sell his fried potatoes.

He gathered his cooking supplies, bought a wagon and hit the road. On route, he passed through Belgium.

While passing through a town fair, he stumbled upon his parents who were giving a performance.

Jean Frédéric set himself up next to them and started selling his deep fried potatoes to everybody at the fair, who ate them happily.

His younger brother was there too, and Jean Frédéric convinced him to sell his deep fried potatoes at other fairs. But it was a difficult job. You had to wake up very early in the morning to peel hundreds of potatoes...

... and cut them into thin slices before cooking them, then sell as many as possible before the end of the day.

One day, Jean Frédéric decided to call his deep fried potatoes... fritz. It was the short form of his German first name (Friedrich) and it sounded just like the French word for fried, *"frite"*!

Since it was faster and more fun than saying deep fried potatoes, people liked going to Fritz's place... to eat some Fritz!

At this time, grease was very expensive and nobody used it to make fries. So, when Fritz arrived in the towns, people were delighted since they didn't have many opportunities to eat fries.

The two brothers were very happy and
spent their time going far and wide
across Belgium selling their fries.

To work more quickly, Jean Frédéric Krieger had an idea: he made a hole in the table and installed a metal grate.

He put the potatoes on the grate and covered
them with a metal sheet, that he tapped with a
hammer: the potatoes fell out in long rectangular
sticks into the bucket underneath the table.

Then he dropped them into boiling grease...

And bam!... the fries that you
know and love were born!

Everyone loved the new shape of the fries you could hold between your fingers.

Jean Frédéric gradually perfected his invention and created the fry cutter, which was even better since it didn't require a hammer.

His very beautiful and intelligent wife
explained to him that he could make
even more money if he sold his fries in...

...a beautiful store rather than in a canvas tent. And this is how more and more rich people started eating fries.

In Belgium, Fritz's fries became so well-known that people came from other countries to try them. Victor Hugo, a famous French writer, loved going to Fritz's place to eat them.

His fries were so popular
even Americans loved them.

Gradually, lots of restaurants started serving fries. But, in Belgium, fries were often eaten on their own, and always with the fingers...

... In France, they were eaten with
grilled meats, and **always** with a fork.

Today, fries are eaten with mayonnaise or ketchup at sit-down or fast food restaurants.

And you can even ask your mom or dad
to make you some at home with a fryer!

And you, what are your favorite

# FRENCH FRIES

?

There you go, now you know everything about the invention of FRENCH FRIES!

But do you remember everything you've read

Play the MEMORY game to see what you remember!

# MEMORY GAME

**1** In which city did Jean Frédéric Krieger discover fries?

**2** In which country did he stop to sell his fries at fairs?

**3** With whom did he sell his fries at these fairs?

**4** What name did Jean Frédéric Krieger give his fried potatoes?

**5** Which famous French writer went to Jean Frédéric Krieger's place to eat fries?

1. Paris
2. Belgium
3. His brother
4. Fritz
5. Victor Hugo

# A FIREFLY BOOK

Published by Firefly Books Ltd. 2016

Source edition © 2015 Les Frites, ÉDITIONS PLAY BAC, 33 rue du Petit-Musc, 75004, Paris, France, 2015

This translated edition copyright © 2016 Firefly Books

First printing

**Publisher Cataloging-in-Publication Data (U.S.)**

Names: Fejtö, Raphaël, author. | Greenspoon, Golda, translator. | Mersereau, Claudine, translator.
Title: French fries / Raphaël Fejtö.
Description: Richmond Hill, Ontario, Canada : Firefly Books, 2016. | Series: Little Inventions | Originally published by Éditions Play Bac, Paris, 2015 as Les p'tites inventions: Les Frites | Summary: "This brief history on one of the small, overlooked inventions we use in our everyday lives, in a six-part series is geared toward children. With fun and quirky illustrations and dialog, it also comes with a memory quiz to ensure children retain what they learn" -- Provided by publisher.
Identifiers: ISBN 978-1-77085-746-9 (hardcover)
Subjects: LCSH: French fries – History -- Juvenile literature.
Classification: LCC TX803.P8F458 |DDC 641.6521 – dc23

**Library and Archives Canada Cataloguing in Publication**

Fejtö, Raphaël
[Frites. English]
    French fries / Raphaël Fejtö.
(Little inventions)
Translation of: Les frites.
ISBN 978-1-77085-746-9 (bound)
    1. French fries--History--Juvenile literature. I. Title. II. Title: Frites. English.
TX803.P8F4613 2016    j641.6'521    C2016-900076-1

Published in the United States by
Firefly Books (U.S.) Inc.
P.O. Box 1338, Ellicott Station
Buffalo, New York 14205

Published in Canada by
Firefly Books Ltd.
50 Staples Avenue, Unit 1
Richmond Hill, Ontario L4B 0A7

Printed in China

*les p'tites inventions*